WORLD WAR
YOU

World War You

Jorge Mesa

Published by Third Eye Edify, 2023.

While every precaution has been taken in the preparation of this book, the publisher assumes no responsibility for errors or omissions, or for damages resulting from the use of the information contained herein.

WORLD WAR YOU

First edition. November 4, 2023.

Copyright © 2023 Jorge Mesa.

Written by Jorge Mesa.

Table of Contents

Title Page 1
Copyright Page 2
Dedication 5
A QUICK NOTE ABOUT THIS BOOK'S FORMAT 6
Preface 8
1 9
2 13
3 16
4 20
5 24
6 27
7 32
8 36
9 38
10 40
11 44
12 46
13 48
14 51
15 54
NOTES 56
NOTES 57
Sign up for Jorge Mesa's Mailing List 58
About the Author 59
About the Publisher 60

———This book is dedicated to the most incredible and supportive person I have ever met, my wife Pétri. She truly is "The Rock" for me and every person that comes into contact with her. I am forever grateful for your LARGER THAN LIFE love and dedication to being truly amazing!———

A QUICK NOTE ABOUT THIS BOOK'S FORMAT

———I did not have an impulse to provide a genuine Table of Contents for this book. There is one provided merely for convenience in the ebook version. My intention is to have ideas broken up into segments that do not require titles. There is simply a numerical separation for each "chapter" in order for there to be stopping points so you can take breaks whenever you need to. Thank you for giving me the opportunity to speak so candidly about so many different topics here in this book. There are also two blank pages labeled "notes" at the very end of this humble little book just in case you want to jot down any thoughts or ideas (or even rebuttals) to anything presented here. Please check out everything else I do in the spirit of this book at ThirdEyeEdify.com and feel free to contact me there with any feedback or even ideas for future podcast episodes or even book concepts! While this is my very first book, it will absolutely not be my last. I hope you gain from reading this book and if so, please share it with others so these messages can be spread to as many people as possible.———

WORLD WAR YOU

Preface

Have you ever even read the works of Copernicus? Standing tall in almost theological excellence with his cunningly coercive yet confident correctitudes. Must Penrose pen such a brand of math that almost no one can honestly find any use in it other than to blindly praise it. Please remind me what a living room at a Super Bowl party and a ceremonious gathering of any religion have in common? Just like a group of seated entertainment seekers at a movie theater or a group of righteously religious families at a church on any holy day, there is no difference in the stoic focus of these possessed patrons. They are all under the same spell. If this doesn't already interest you then please refer to one of life's most important and persistent lessons...do not judge a book by its cover. It is finally time to dismantle history (HIS story) and firmly plant the mystery (MY story).

It remains a vivid memory. I was still enjoying the relative simplicity of a life that had not yet graduated into double digits. There I sat, engorging my saturated senses as I prepped for an already quite familiar minute or two with My Fellow Americans as we all clapped, roared and applauded (and a bit of chuckling) for the on-screen death of yet another evil villain from yet another cookie cutter concoction that HOLYwood put out for all of us to feed our precious light to. Yet another ramblingly excessive and beyond coincidentally repetitive bit of programming to aid us in our culturally inculcated need for vegging out approximately 90 minutes at a time. All of this, as is cinematically customary, was preceded by a quick "heart to heart" where the "villain" gets a chance to let it all out and show that He or She was actually a real human being all along. An actual real life human being with thoughts and feelings that at times may even resemble your own. This may be hard to take in all at once but the very same people that take a different side on certain things in the world, politically racially or otherwise, are also real life, actual human beings just like you.

    A young child looking forward to the killing of a human being on a big screen amidst a crowd of people who are visibly thirsty for blood is socially manipulative at best and was supposed to be a relic of a bygone era found only in history books to be read about and studied in order to never repeat it. Just like our parents, however, you will always take something from your heritage whether it is a certain social tendency or perhaps the way your father laughs. Humans tend to exemplify certain traits they may not normally find reasonable while in a mob mentality and *entertainment* is one of the most effective ways of getting a large number of people to agree on something and even immediately feel impassioned to die fighting for it without ever meeting the masterminds behind it. One need not look further than the push for a big breakfast in the early twentieth century when countless "doctors" were led to advertise it as an absolute necessity to the average working Woman or Man just to sell more bacon. Fast forward to the 1970's until present and you now have a devolution (DEVILution) of nutrition for an average teenage breakfast to merely consist of a dastardly combination of heavily pasteurized baby cow food and a big bowl of "part of a balanced breakfast." A substance that has such little value beyond its branding that it is almost a joke to call it food, and this is before we even begin to discuss how poisonous a non-nutritious food like breakfast cereal is or whether other countries are even allowed to sell them.

 Since the instauration of our wonderful entertainment industry, the Occidental nations (and some Oriental as well) have seen a rapid decline in our ability to experience the very world we live in for what it is. Most important of which may just be our relationships to each other and ourselves. There is a WAR within YOU right now and YOU did absolutely nothing to start it. No assassination, no false flags, no sanctions, no explosions. You've been convinced by the very entertainment you think you need or even deserve since your very first taste of it, that you should exist a certain way. Convinced you should live like movie stars do, or more importantly that you would even get the chance. You've been convinced that you must "seize your moment, no matter what it takes." Convinced that "nice guys finish last." Convinced that you can easily live an "own it now, pay for it later" lifestyle. Convinced that you no longer need to retain a whole library of information in your beautiful mind because all you need now is a well charged cellular telephone with an internet connection complete with a monthly "transhuman tax." If the phone dies....does your entire spiritual being die with it? More importantly, is your entire being now attached to this pocket computer at a cellular (no pun intended) level? Anyone reading this who is old enough to remember can easily attest to the simple fact that life **CAN** exist without these menacingly bulky blocks of technology in our pockets. Could you picture yourself existing for 24 hours without even thinking about that phone or is it already well past that, is it now actually a part of you?! How many times have you clicked "AGREE" in the last 20 or so years without reading even one word of said contract? Have we been tricked to willingly become cyborgs? Have we been tricked into most of our daily rituals?

 NO!! You as a human being are far more powerful than you were led to believe. When your mother or father told you that "you can be anything you want to be" they were almost right. Starting your life without adding pedallic bloodletting and poison needles for an extra fee the moment you are born would have helped. Maybe after we stop these things, and maybe even get proper nutrition from day one, can we finally see a human grow up and work their way back into being able to afford their lives. Perhaps we can actually kick start generations of children who are able to think for themselves and acknowledge the precious and natural intuition that guides us through our lives without being trained to question it at every turn.

    What exactly do we do to afford anything? What exactly is wealth in our common definition. What is luxury? — According to the famous 19th Century German Composer Richard Wagner in his book "The Art-Work of The Future" luxury is: "...as heartless, inhuman, insatiable, and egoistic as the 'need' which called it forth, but which, with all its heaping-up and over-reaching, it never more can still. For this need itself is no natural and therefore satisfiable one; by very reason that, being false, it has no true, essential antithesis in which it may be spent, consumed, and satisfied." It is more alluring than any shiny electric HOV lane approved Sedan. It is more seductive than any 5 star dessert. It is the thing that keeps our now needy minds content for at least a few seconds at a time in our daily existence. It is a never-ending flow of warm running water in a shower. It is a Thai restaurant that also serves Japanese food in the middle of London. It is coffee "brewed" from a pod and it is something that we are just going to have to unlearn lest we fall victim to it like our most recent ancestry.

    I always thought it was relatively surprising when someone I met or an acquaintance of mine had either no interest or a genuine lack of knowledge when it came to video games or even my favorite hockey team. It's always more, more, more....NOW 32% MORE!! (Than all other leading brands©), and its all a meaningless, empty LUXURY. I was never against anyone who didn't follow my specific passions during those earlier years of my life but I also thought nothing of it. I thought nothing of how little the majority of humans in this seemingly limitless expanse we call Earth shared almost anything with my daily SUPERSIZED United States life. Now looking back I can only feel lucky at the opportunity to speak on the other side of this. I was supposed to be a victim of all of this luxury. I was supposed to become some kind of computer whiz working for NASA or perhaps a hacker working for the CIA. I was raised and trained by a system that was banking on me becoming an almost computer terminal-like part of that very same system. A trained animal ready to strike at whatever reality TV style nonsense they wanted me to get a reaction from. Perhaps they wanted me to become a teacher that would aimlessly follow whatever Department of Education vomit they had prepared for that generation of higher learning. It didn't work. *I am not a computer and neither are you.* Computers, and other technologies like them, can certainly be used to help us do some interesting and very useful things but as of right now, they are being used to inhibit our ability to become the unbelievably limitless and powerful humans we are all meant to be.

When I was in grade school in the 1980's and 90's our entire class was taught to type with the QWERTY keyboard system. Now, our youth isn't even shown proper typing technique. The assumption here is very clear, your voice is all you need and your touch screen is all you'll ever need. This may seem like a technological evolution but how many times have you craved a button to press or a keyboard to type with in the newest iterations of this technology? What is the goal? To make sure that it becomes less and less convenient to do exactly what you want with these modern computers and have far less control over what you can and cannot do. Saving a photo? Don't worry, it's on the cloud. What is the file name? DON'T WORRY ABOUT IT! No internet connection? NO PHOTO! This is cause for concern on many levels which I will bring to light, along with many other things, in this book.

2

There are people right now who are convinced they are trans...no, no...NOT transsexual but TRANSHUMAN. This very sad and thankfully avoidable fate for most of humanity will take a whole lot of work and "de-programming" to rise above, but we can do it. A knife can either be used to cut a wedding cake or it can used for things that are much worse and it's up to the person holding the knife to make good decisions. Computers are exactly the same, and to think that humans are supposed to be "evolving" into a new human/machine hybrid should be one of the most terrifying things you have read up until now in this little book. Is there a cell phone near you right now? Is there a cell phone in your pocket right now? Is there a cell phone right next to your brain as you sleep? That little computer is the first very large step to molding you into something much different than what our incredible species can become if we are only given the chance. Before these mini computers, these "fondle slabs," these "black mirrors" were essentially mandated on the technological world, people used to actually K N O W things. If asked for a family members' phone number or address, most people had these things memorized with no battery life or wifi signal needed. Knowledge on all kinds of topics, memorization of countless ideas and facts were on tap just because we were given the opportunity to put our perplexingly fantastic brains to use. Nowadays, it is quite commonplace to hear something along the lines of:

"I don't need to K N O W it...I can just **Google** it." This is currently an unfortunate success of the powers that should not be.

What happens if that little computer is not charged?! What happens if that little box filled with lithium and other things that are hardly abundant in most of our world and potentially cause wars, what happens if you "don't have any signal?" Do you also lose all of your knowledge? Are you still you? Are you already transhuman? Are you a cyborg? Are you already what THEY want you to be?

We are trained to accept our current historical texts and teachings that 2,000, or even 4,000 years ago our species was in a primitive state of knowledge that didn't even have the ability to dress themselves and yet...pyramids (healthy frequency generators), running water (NOT locally recycled sewage), free energy, magnetic levitation tools, permaculture and a potential web of information flowing freely in the aether for all connected minds to communicate with (the original internet) existed. Are we truly expected to believe that these generations upon generations of humans throughout our realm were fools because they believed the earth stood still as the perpetually moving *Skyclock* provided useful information they used throughout the year; are we truly expected to believe that they could not eat without a supermarket? Are we going to let whoever choses to do so, Rockefeller or Globalists or whatever label you feel like giving your flavor of the week to blame, give us a false history that immediately falls apart as soon as you take it upon yourself to glance just beyond the first layer?

    Education used to be a very different thing regardless of whether or not you were rich or poor. After reading countless books that required translation because they were either written in a language other than my own or because the author was educated so much more thoroughly than we are today that they wrote entire books in Latin just because they could (or because it was the easiest way to keep it out of reach for us mere peasants), it is becoming more and more clear that something is wrong with a large portion how we are raised. Our parents hardly had a chance to raise us like they would have wanted to or perhaps thought they could. They had to work and during those peak hours, if they were lucky enough to have a M-F 9-5, they had no choice but to hand over their beautiful young children to our state funded indoctrination camps that made sure we were all ready to compete with each other and have 2 or 3 jobs to make sure college was achievable regardless of whether or not that degree would do anything for them except create yet another slave to this horrid system of usury. Hand your children off to this state run insanity, hand them off to facilities that could easily act like prisons for fourteen years and see if you think they are ready to live in the real world. Were all the gaps of parental tutelage, thanks to your forced need to work in the hamster wheel, filled by the Department of Education? Ask yourself this before denouncing a home schooling family who sees nothing but negativity and an improper education coming from *The System*. Make sure you actually understand the ethos of an Amish community before you laugh off their lifestyle amidst our miserable modern insanity. They probably contribute more for your community than your *tax dollars* or your *government*...

3

Do you know what time it is? Please, no phones or computers or televisions or analog/digital clocks of any kind. Is the time of 17:42:28 an actual thing in nature? Perhaps we could quantify seconds by our sky but it would seem irrelevant. Unless of course you become convinced by either decades of indoctrination camp (public school), some good old TV broad**casting** (spell casting) or by your parents (not their fault) that you should live a life of servitude where every "hour" of time worked away from your family, away from your household, friends and neighbors is required to justify your existence. Where the need to compete with every fellow human being you've ever met, regardless of your relationship, is paramount to your "success." On top of that, every precious moment outside of this "job" you will be enticed to *relax* and maybe even have some *fun* with social media, movies, video games or intoxicants. This of course will take even more precious time away from your family before you hit your pillow with its 7 month old unwashed pillowcase for the night.

 What exactly does a life like that lead to? Firstly, you'll be overworked, underpaid and unwilling to dare a different path. Secondly, and perhaps most importantly, you'll be unable to discover what genuine and beautifully unique gifts you have to offer this world. This should be the grand ethos of all human beings! Instead, an extremley large majority of us are locked into some sadistic rhythm that we cannot either explain or control. A rhythm you'll never have the *time* to evolve into your personal mastery or ever legitimately click into place. Perhaps this is one reason that video games are now grossing more per year than film and sports COMBINED. This is to the point where people will gladly watch other people play rather than bother to play themselves and this may end up being discussed more thoroughly in another chapter or perhaps a whole entire separate book.

 Is this something we "evolved" into naturally? Would a species as clearly powerful and strong willed as Human Beings truly succumb to such a life of destitute drudgery? A human would *never* get to this point without having someone or something push them or coerce them towards that type of life. This life which is said to be a meaningless drift though a potentially endless and ever-expanding void while we all play the role of randomly evolved space monkeys on a spinning, molten filled oblate spheroid. Whether or not those theories hold to be true is another story. The real story here is that human intelligence is in a red zone with regard to its devolution. How else would parents across the globe ever choose a computer or television over a human life? Why would any one of us work so often that our children would not only require babysitting (whether by human or computer) but an entire program of education which takes them away from the ones they love most and the ones they can learn the most from when it comes to several important facets of this incredible world.

    I used to think of this as a comment made in haste: "I never use any of that crap from grade school." I immediately think of how many college graduates have yet to perform ANY actual work in their prospective fields throughout the entirety of their post graduate schooling. I think about how grade school, at the very least, provided a largely unique and diverse group of people to meet and interact with. I know what I *did* get from the Department of Education curriculum. I am also finally becoming quite aware of what I *did not* get from the D.O.E. as well as all of the hidden "perks" that were skillfully sprinkled into my education. I also acknowledge that certain teachers make sure certain things end up in their classroom whether or not it was on their syllabus. I am grateful for anyone who takes an honest and loving approach to absolutely any vocation ESPECIALLY the education of children.

    Think about how much time you have missed out on in your child's life. If you're not a parent, then place it in the context of your family or simply your overall work/life balance. No matter how old, think about how much time was spent actually helping the Federal Reserve and making sure you were spending money while also taking money from anyone and everything imaginable. How much money did you spend with companies that actually care about what they make, how they make it and where they make it. Even certain baby foods created by caring parents and doctors roll through some companies predetermined ingredient/additive/warning labels etcetera, etcetera, etcetera. Even now as I am creating this tome of thoughts for you dear reader to take in, I see dotted red lines and other corrections by the very word processor I am using. I write out etc. as etcetera and there is no indication to correct this. I've never really typed out this word before but I have seen its original form. The reason to mention this is that we have almost every facet of our physical and digital lives overseen by some force whether it is a governing body or some binary algorithm staring you dead in the face every time you open a computer, phone, smartwatch, smart TV smart toaster...whatever. You can't even type a word without some kind of device analyzing it, even if it is merely to check the spelling. Once you click or press or say "AGREE" everything that occurs on that platform from that moment on is essentially fair game in the open market of the "Internet of Things." Did you want good old movie shops to go belly up? Was it your intention to let restaurants, farms, retail stores and many more lose their ability to do business because you lost your ability to shop outside of your bathroom?

    I have ironically been focusing on education more now that I'm out of that system and due to the mandatory system of online learning that has been forced on almost every child in the world recently. It seems as if how we are taught and who is led to teach us has changed dramatically ever since the turn of the 20th Century. Once we began to film our realm (and once central banks were firmly back in the drivers seat for much of the world) education began to take a much different shape in overall style, delivery and substance. Ever since around 2001 there has been a much more drastic shift in what we are supposed to consider education. Now, more than ever, it is time to do OUR part in making sure we get the following generations to steer clear of this path that has so imminently placed our species in more danger than anyone could have ever planned against.

    If there is one aspect of education that could potentially be tackled head on before anything else I would hope it would be the implementation of digital/robotic devices and services. I used to think that video games, to label them broadly, would be a very useful way for children to learn. I was certain that because I felt like I gained something from the games I played that anyone would indeed be able to take advantage of this as a tool for good. Looking back I am saddened to realize that this simply is not true on many levels. Rather than make an entire book starting from this concept lets just put it in plain language. When you allow a robot of any kind to do the work of a human being, the parties involved almost immediately change their mind about the REAL world. I'm not standing here claiming that watching an old episode of your favorite show from the past is going to absolutely bring someone to quit their job and hate their life and push themselves to homelessness. Our modern version of functioning society is already providing that service. I'm discussing something much deeper. Something that cannot be described with words alone. Perhaps the easiest way to describe it is LOVE. By allowing certain movies or games to become mainstays in people's lives they not only become attached and even comforted by the images but they may even feel something along the lines of actual love for it. I know I have. I've truly loved a few video games and movies in my life. I have had "long term relationships" with games for almost all of my life. I would give uninterrupted attention and patience to some of these creations and there were no people in sight for hours. Just my brightly glowing television and me. Video images and broadcasting by way of television or computer screens are absolutely 100% doing a disservice to our brains regarding development and overall learning ability.

One of the very clearest memories from my early schooling (Kindergarten here in the West) was a teacher explaining to us what rocket ships needed to be made out of in order for them to successfully re-enter the Earth's atmosphere. Why in the world would that be a focus of my First Grade, fresh out of Kindergarten education? Why wasn't I being shown how soil works? Why wasn't there a larger focus on how vast and incredible our world is and how people from all of our known continents have such different lives and values and that they are ALL valid and wonderful ways to live and enjoy our place here on Earth. Why wasn't I shown that Disney had "retired" Nazis making little cartoony depictions of space travel well before it had ever happened and how come Werner Von Braun himself then speaks to us about his "vision of the future" while writing books about a person name Elon governing the future human civilization that would eventually end up on Mars well before a real life person named Elon took it upon himself to purchase "free speech" for BILLIONS of USD and then confusingly change that platform's name to "X?"

   Yet another very early memory of my schooling included explanations about how the earlier and much more poorly educated "fools" that made up our ancestry didn't realize that the earth was not flat and that it is indeed a sphere that was SPINNING, ORBITING and FLYING simultaneously at speeds that are absolutely incomprehensible to us. This, of course, is happening while people are walking upside down across the globe and as planes land perfectly on runways that align North to South (think about it). If that were true then let me ask you dear reader, would Orion's belt still be in the same exact orientation that the pyramids at Giza were created to align with? And while we're on the topic of speeds and distances that are relatively incalculable based on sights you will never see with you own eyes unless *you yourself* were to embark on a journey into space, I specifically recall many discussions in school on invisible enemies that are far too small to see with our own eyes that are EVERYWHERE and constantly attempting to enter your very capable and healthy bodies in order to kill you. G E R M S!!! I was always worried and yet, I knew something was wrong. "How did we make it this far?" I frequently thought to myself, somehow understanding that it was not best to think it out loud. I would leave school, look up at the sun and almost immediately think "HOW?!!? How is that burning coin in the sky THAT FAR AWAY?" my curious little mind thought to itself.

Regardless, I was still so fascinated and ready to tackle the mystery that I, along with many of my miniature peers, was quite willing to heed the call and become an astronaut myself. I could see things many have not and maybe even help unravel the innumerable riddles of the universe. There was no shortage of alien programming on cable television in the 80's and 90's so on top of having unachievable fantasies, I was completely engrossed in a world that I can only now confidently label as fiction at best. I talked about it all the time in my youth and, much like I lamented earlier, I was quickly molding into a potential candidate for a hopeless NASA cubicle critter completely oblivious to my surroundings and my actual REALITY. The frustrating reality is that there are still PLENTY of mysteries to unravel right here in our wonderful shared space we call home before we need to theorize about terraforming Mars with nukes!

The hits kept coming as school progressed and I suddenly found myself obsessed with Dinosaurs. I knew ALL of the names, I studied the etymology, I knew which dinosaurs lived in which periods and I diligently studied the ancient pre-extinction habitats and all of the things that came with it. All of this was passionately pursued without the nudging or guidance of my own prescription strength K-12 education. I learned about the eschatological nature of their extinction and I had a distinct drive for it that was all my own...or so I thought. Perhaps there was an overload of advertisements, perhaps they were all over children's programming just like they are today.

On the other side of this vast and exciting world of knowledge, the information that was purposefully kept from me were things such as: when was the first set of dinosaur bones discovered? Do museums actually have real dinosaur bones on display? Why are we suddenly assuming that all dinosaurs had feathers? Why are T-Rex's arms COMPLETELY USELESS?! I'll leave the sleuthing to you, should you wish to do so, but please allow me to continue because the last few minutes may have a felt a bit bitter and potentially quite tough to swallow for the uninitiated. Maybe I am just a little bitter.

Maybe I feel like I'm in a race and I completely missed the opening bell placing me half a mile behind my potential. Maybe that was the point. Maybe the very English language I was raised with which seems so distant in context, usability and learning curve was meant to keep me in the dark about so many things that I would never flourish like we humans are meant to.

Bitterness is not the impetus for this book, my goal is to edify through curiosity. My true wish here is to open eyes and maybe even a few third eyes too. YOU are bombarded with inputs of all kinds everywhere you go and as soon as you cross the line that I and many others have crossed in the past twenty or so years, your perception of the world changes dramatically almost overnight. These "inputs" this "sensory overload" can actually be ignored and therefore immediately powerless. This constant bombardment can be easily overcome with far less effort than you may think, even if it does indeed mean completely changing the approach to your daily life regardless of what you do for work, love, family, leisure etcetera.

I've read a very large amount of books lately that, while providing me with much desired information and insight to either a particular topic or time period, were almost always written with a specific type of audience in mind, a predictably small audience relatively speaking. A huge percentage of these books essentially required a solid foundation of knowledge prior to reading it or at the very least an open mind towards topics that were either highly controversial or written in such a way that most people wouldn't even bother with it. This book you hold now, I truly believe, is a noble and valid attempt to bring something to the table for both sides of this proverbial coin. I want to reach people who are already engrossed in the type of research I am to take a step back and see how far they've come and to hopefully see where they stand compared to someone like myself who has seen so much change in my life so far. I, perhaps more importantly, also want to reach people who are potentially unaware of, or manipulated to see right past, all of the things that surround you on a daily basis. The title of this book implies malicious intent from the powers that should not be and that is something that needs to be shown. However, the true goal here is to hopefully show you, dear reader, things that have been intentionally kept from your beautiful mind and yet right out in the open for all to see. This is the power of language. This is the power of symbology and that is just the tip of this humongous iceberg.

Let's take a moment to discuss gender. This is not going to be a discussion on the current gender confusion that is exploding in the West and as far as I can tell, the rest of the world. I am very specifically referring to the English language and at a much more esoteric level, the SUN and MOON. Without entering into a discussion I will save for further in this book, why is it that our precious English language, which is somehow the current international language of diplomacy, does not imply gender like the rest of the world? Why do some languages read in the opposite direction (right to left or perhaps we will call it WEST or maybe even NORTH depending on how you see things)? Are you aware that we actually have much in common with Sanskrit, one of our historical narratives earliest written alphabets? Are you aware of how similar Sanskrit, Greek, Hebrew, Celtic and English are? If we are to assume that most humans write with their right hand (write hand), although many people ancient and modern are known to write quite well with either hand, when we write the English language (left to right or EAST or potentially SOUTH) we are actually writing AWAY from our heart. These other languages are actually writing TOWARDS their heart. Which one sounds more appropriate to you? Why does it seem like we are ALL OF A SUDDEN beholden to this English language which actually has far less ways to express itself than others. There is a type of language that transcends all of this. If you immediately thought Music or Math or Love then you are at least thinking the right way but I am speaking very specifically about Symbology, the language of symbols. You are BOMBARDED with symbols every single second of every waking moment you experience in your life. Then, once you go to sleep and have a dream...more symbols, *everywhere*. Egyptian language is written in pictures or what we call hieroglyphs. Characters from some Southeast Asian languages are pictorial in nature. Every single letter we used in the English language is a symbol. Look at capitol 'N' and capitol 'H.' They are both composed of two parallel lines with one having a perfectly centered and horizontal bridge while the other has a diagonal bridge. They also both start with a very similar sound. This is the power of symbology, not these distinct concepts but the fact that a very large portion of people reading this have never taken the time to analyze even the simplest of things they see regularly and understand it at a very deep subconscious level.

We should also mention Hebrew here, which shares over 500 root words with Sanskrit, because they have 2 versions of their written language. One with vowels and one without. Once someone is ready they can actually read the original Torah with merely consonants and the vowels are understood. The Torah (and Bible) are actually meant to be sung from memory and that is a whole other topic for potentially a whole other book! Picture this sentence: WE ALL OVERCAME A HUGE HURDLE. Now without vowels: W LL VRCM A HG HRDL.

I did not sit down and choose some perfect example to make my point here, but please have a good look at it. If you put the time into it and studied English in this very particular way, you could eventually decipher it. English is also a completely different language that was not made for that style of written interpretation so there is going to be more than enough of an argument that removing vowels from our modern English language doesn't always work perfectly in this way. Picture your standard airport arrivals/departures bulletin board though. All of the airports are typically abbreviated: LGA, LAX etc. We don't even have to ask which is which, we immediately understand the *symbolic* representation.

A language that has been created with this "vowelless" or "consonantary" writing style is called **Abjad** or **West Semitic**. There are other terms that have been used to describe this writing style but this is enough info for you to do your own research on this vast subject. An important observation to make here is that when we speak or sing as human beings, the vowels are where we place our "notes." To put it another way, you cannot sing the letter 'T' there simply must be a vowel before or after it to bring any official meaning or response from the listener. So to be clear, regardless of Abjad's usage and application, vowels **are** indeed needed for spoken language.

We diverged slightly but this is the nature of having an unquenchable drive towards knowledge. We are all built this way, but regardless of whatever we want to label this huge force that is pushing against us physically AND spiritually it seems especially clear that in the last few years, and many centuries of planning leading up to that, there has been an attempt to rid our species of the need to think. To rid our species of the desire to reproduce. To rid our species of its tireless pursuit of a more grand and rewarding connection with nature, with the world we were born into, with the world that we are here to unravel together. I am speaking of a world that can only be labeled as transhuman. Every moment you spend aimlessly grabbing at some social media dopamine hit or some pointless reward in a video game you are spending less and less time as the human being you were meant to be. Perhaps you are not one of the "100,000 or so people with a brain chip" to quote Dennis Bushnell of NASA but having something like a cell phone in your pocket or a smartwatch on your wrist is dragging you farther and farther away from anything resembling your actual human self.

———"Accordingly you won't wonder any more that a very excellent order of sounds or pitches in a musical system or scale has been set up by men, since you see that they are doing nothing else in this business except to play the apes of God the Creator and to act out, as it were, a certain drama of the ordination of the celestial movements."———

Johannes Kepler from "The Harmonies of the World" 1619

• • • •

What does this quote mean to you? I'm certain almost anyone would have broadly varying answers. Most curious to me are two things, "...wondering if a musical system has been set up by men..." and "...a certain drama of the ordination of the celestial movements." The book that this quote comes from is quite provocative and is mysteriously left as an oft forgotten memory of only a learned few. Perhaps, however, you remember a humongous telescope named the Kepler Space Telescope which was recently retired. Curiosity can lead to much discovery all by itself and the person who this telescope is named after was clearly well educated and undeniably curious. Questioning whether or not man created music is an extremely lengthy and potentially open ended topic but in the case of this particular question, Kepler is of the opinion that man certainly did not create it but merely found a way to manipulate it. Much like Nikola Tesla with his Rotating Magnetic Wheel, he did not invent it but was fully aware that he simply discovered what nature provided. Unfortunately, this "manipulation" of nature's gift of music is severely crippling to the true potential of *music* or whatever it is that you would like to call the the intelligent and informed technical control of frequency(ies) by voice or instrument. No true potential can ever be finally extracted from whatever we want to label music as but the current *Equal Temperament* (every musical note is exactly the same mathematical distance from the next, think of piano keys) that Western Music Theory brings us is clearly manipulated in such a way that we end up only being able to use a small part of it's grand spectrum. To make a clear example, everyone knows there are limitless colors in our visible spectrum and frequency is no different. As a matter of fact, our hearing senses are one of the very first things that develops in the womb and the hearing spectrum we posses is tenfold of what our eyes can effectively see. This is a bold statement, but we have a genuine obligation to think as far outside of the box as possible in our current existence. We are either transitioning from one age to another or finding ourselves right smack in the middle of a new age. The "internet" of the human consciousness is absolutely active and we are more powerful than we were ever led to believe by the powers that should not be (or never were). There is a very high probability in my opinion that **ALL** human beings can communicate at some psycho-spiritual level. This would be a crucial transition point for the known world and you'd be lying to yourself if you said that this has never crossed your instinctually inquisitive and beautiful mind for even a fledgeling moment.

 My life's work was officially undetermined until I was a mid-teen youngster looking for work I was good at that was fun and also giving me a chance to be a teacher while also getting to see lots of "cool" places and meet tons of people. Music, for the most part, fits this criteria except of course for a few unforeseen consequences of this type of life-long sacrifice. A few short years ago we all experienced yet another attempt to completely enslave humanity as *yet another* "global pandemic" reared its ugly head again in 2020 except this time "they" were playing for a chance to make it to the final round of the playoffs. Being a working musician in ANY capacity was completely affected by this and I was immediately forced to reflect with a focused fervor towards just what, exactly, I was going to do to create the kind of life for my family that would lead to the most rewarding way to learn from and live with this wonderful Earth while still providing food and shelter.

 I really and truly am a musician. Here's the other part of that...so are YOU, dear reader. Every human being on this planet is absolutely 100% an honest to goodness musician. Perhaps we will label the untrained musicians out there *honest musicians*. Think of it this way, the moral of the story when reading "The Emperor's New Clothing" is clear; when seeing the world through the eyes of a child, the obvious once again becomes obvious. In regards to something as intuitive as listening to music, whether or not you actually are a card carrying trained musician, you will have an opinion about it. More succinctly, if something sounds "wrong" or "out of tune" YOU, dear reader, will be able to make this distinction whether or not you have the skills and requirements to analyze and teach the many potential reasons why. This isn't about being able to play a Trombone on day one or even to sing an Opera after 10 years of hard work. This is about every single human being's innate ability to either understand the intrinsic qualities of how the chords and melodies interact and produce **rhythm** or simply how well of a natural ability all humans have to not only be able to describe the music they are listing to (with or without studied music knowledge or it's appropriate terms) but also to know when something sounds "wrong" or perhaps a better description would be "out of place."

This, if I may, also makes YOU a scientist. You can analyze and potentially describe, without a professional skillset of this particular branch of science's "lingo," the music you hear and even the quality of a performance. All the adults (wage slaves) in "The Emperor's New Clothing" simply ignored their own beautiful and perfect human senses when it came to their immediate and visible reality regarding the Emperor's incredible new outfit. The very reason they ignored it was deviously simple:

————"The whole town knew about the cloth's peculiar power, and all were impatient to find out how stupid their neighbors were."————

-From *Hans Christian Andersen* "Emperor's new Clothing" 1837-

This is not the quote you will often see from this incredible short story written by someone who was clearly in the know, but it almost fully describes the entirety of the moral. This little nugget gave everyone a preconceived notion about what to expect and only when a child had the courage, or perhaps it was just a kid being a kid, to speak out loudly about the true nature of his reality did everyone finally see the obvious as once again obvious.

This perception of right and wrong is very delicate in all of us especially regarding a more esoteric or spiritual truth. This idea of right and wrong can easily slip into another scale of good or bad, day taking turns with night, Yin and Yang or even GOOD vs. EVIL. More on that particular topic later but the main point to take away here is that there should be a higher truth that is inherently right, correct and honest; where "Law and Order" does not have the answer. When it comes to music however, there may be alarming non-truths that shall simply be labeled here as malicious at best.

For most cultures, music is revered as a pure necessity. Aside from the myriad of ways that it is performed for everything from annual celebrations to daily rituals, most of it can be classified as relatively simple at its core. This simplicity guarantees every single person involved can participate. Now let me ask you this, whether you are a well studied musician or not, do you think that all of these different countries and cultures rely on the same exact notes or what we should call pitches (MUSIC SYSTEM to re-quote Kepler a few paragraphs earlier) in their music? Do you think they all use the same musical scales to convey their melodies? The answer, I assume you've already surmised, is quite complicated. In order to bring this concept to the table and to spare the mathematical density of frequency relationships and general music theory, please allow me to share some insight I've gained being a career musician and the proud owner of a brain that simply will not leave me alone.

All of the notes or pitches of our music here in "The West" are subdivided completely equally. A simple watered down example is that the distance from A-B musically speaking, is the same mathematical distance as D-E. This in theory sounds like a very good idea and an obvious choice if we are to even approach being able to quantify what music truly is and how it works by using any instrument other than the absolutely most versatile instrument in the world: The Human Voice. We hear a LOT of different pitches, or frequencies if you like (and also timbres), during our daily lives no matter what we choose to do each day. Even if you were to sit on your couch all day and night you would at least catch a constant *hum* from the fridge or maybe a close proximity computer or perhaps when a shower is running and you can hear that constant sound of water traveling through the pipe or perhaps you are driving and the car itself has noises and even a horn which has a certain pitch when used. I'd love to quote someone like Nikola Tesla right now but I really don't have a genuine source of where he said this and I can only hope it is a gesture of trust to you that I do not claim to know if this is exactly Nikola Tesla since I don't have the source somewhere besides online. The quote is something along the lines of "If you want to know the secrets of the universe, think in terms of frequency and energy." I'm paraphrasing here but every single one of us should be taking a step back from all of the things we think we know about the world works and affirm that you only KNOW what you KNOW. If you don't do something yourself or see something for yourself then take a good moment or two to at least to see another side of the story. The whole point of this book you are now holding is to have everyone who is reading it to be *thinking* about its contents and hopefully, his or her own reality.

Back to this equal subdivision of musical notes, every single key on a piano is the same musical distance from each other no matter where it is located. Again, this sounds like the only obvious approach to creating an instrument. We immediately come across a large number of problems with this but most importantly is how *unnatural* it is. That hum from your fridge and that bird singing outside your window in the morning, no instrument can truly mimic those notes or melodies or whatever sounds you hear. This is nothing to lose sleep over right? Not if you are in a rock band or casually singing at your local church, but as soon as you try to abruptly inject this *forced* musical system into *nature* (the only thing that should matter in our current computer driven insanity), you are absolutely going against the beautiful and natural state of essentially everything in this world. In other words, we are constantly stuck trying to stick a square peg in a round hole when it comes to how we are taught to learn or to simply hear music. More importantly YOUR REALITY IS DISTORTED. Almost all of the topics covered in this book will end up with this mantra. It's an unfortunate truth but it must be brought to light. All of our lives depend on it in my humble opinion.

7

―――"There are only the Male and Female gender existing in all things. Even in music there is a balance between *Major (Male)* and *Minor (Female)*. Each scale has major and minor elements which include intervals and chords. Each chord has a major and a minor component within it as well. It cannot be avoided and it is an immutable law of *nature*. There are two genders and *nature* does not see it any other way."―――

    Jorge Mesa Host of the Third Eye Edify Podcast and the Author of this very book you are now reading. *Written during proofreading in 2023.*

• • • •

Shouldn't we consider the Sun and Moon Male and Female? Let's not argue over which is which right now. Knowing the level of deceptive inversions we are force fed from birth I think it is best to let more future discoveries of our existence answer that for us. In the meantime, let us hypothetically think of the Sun and Moon as the Anode and Cathode of a modern galvanic cell battery. Also, please allow me to produce an obvious rebuttal to one thing right away. Regardless of whether or not we use a particular robot or digital device for good, there will always be one thing keeping it from being the perfect tool and that is energy. A charged battery or a constant source of power is required for any of those things to work. We as humans have a similar predicament but it is quite different to discuss sleeping versus charging a cellular telephone. If we treat our bodies right and have a good life-sleep-eating ratio we are almost limitless to a certain degree.

    Perhaps it is a good time to revisit the very idea of a battery. Since almost anything in the entire world can be likened to one or more things that occur naturally in our very own incredible human bodies, it is worth mentioning that we have some kind of battery-type mechanism available to us. We can instinctively recharge it and even place it into "power save mode" when needed. We apparently cannot fully explain our own bodies recharging mechanism yet through modern science, and it may be worth noting that science can be successfully performed by ANYONE especially in the realm of discovery. The unfortunate truth is that even when science overcomes a world wide problem or finally answers a burning age-old question, history is indeed written by the winners and there are plenty of very frightening stories regarding some of the greatest minds throughout the ages and how they were either stopped in their tracks, jailed or even murdered to keep certain technologies away from the public. Knowledge or KNOWING (KING) is not only power but it can easily be used against someone without them ever becoming aware of it.

Batteries, after a relatively rudimentary search, will show to have been invented merely 200 or so years before the writing of this book. Those of you more deeply rooted in this type of information will find no surprise in The Royal Society's involvement in this huge step forward for humanity. If The Royal Society is currently unfamiliar to you please go and look them up. They have backed some of the largest paradigm-shifting changes in recent history and that alone is worth keeping them on your radar. Here we will credit Alessandro Giuseppe Antonio Anastasio Volta, the word VOLT is of course named after him and with it, the concept of voltage. This battery apparently debunked the theory that electricity could only be generated by living beings.

Does anything exist that doesn't require a charge up of some kind? Can anything "work" without using up stored energy? Is there anything on Earth that acts in perpetual motion? Take a moment, dear reader, and go look up the concept of perpetual motion if you are not already familiar. If you are indeed acclimated to this subject, please take another moment and see whether or not any living human being is allowed to create a patent for a "Perpetual Motion Machine." I think you might be as surprised as I was to discover that the answer is a resounding NO.

Why in the world would there be restrictions on what our limitless minds and hard work can potentially create? No way, no how; you are absolutely NOT allowed to dare to even attempt to bother creating something as impossible and frivolous and wasteful as a device of this nature. Who would want limitless free energy? Who would want to prevent such a thing? Why aren't we allowed, or at least encouraged, to try?! This is a large amount of heavy questions but to answer most of them simply, it would seem as if the people making these decisions for us are clearly against it for reasons that I can only assume are NOT in our best interests as a species. What of Satellites? What of the Earth in our currently accepted heliocentric model? What of Niagara Falls? Do these things not move endlessly without fail or need for further energy sources? Perhaps I'm removing us a bit from where we were going but at least think about this, there are some satellites amongst the 13,000+ (over 23,000 objects overall) currently in orbit according to the United Nations OSOidx (Outer Space Object Index) that have been active since the late 50's! Satellites created and sent into LEO (Low Earth Orbit) from either Russia, the United States or elsewhere are potentially floating right above our heads and still functioning perfectly with no physical contact, repair or anything of that nature for well over 50 years. How many things can you think of that were made so perfectly as to not require any maintenance and still work as intended after that long? If one of them failed would it finally land on the Earth with a resounding THUD as if it were the final note of some huge symphonic masterpiece? The Earth does spin endlessly according to what we are told to accept as fact. Is this kind of technology something we can eventually mimic on a much smaller scale? Have we already succeeded and lost it to history? Regardless of what you believe, the Earth or the ceiling of stars above us are all moving in perpetuity and never stop. This is the definition of Perpetual Motion. Can we not at least attempt to reproduce this in nature, in our very own realm? Have we now been successfully trained to look DOWN at our screens with not even a precious moment to take the time to look UP and think for ourselves regarding what we see and feel in our hearts? Just like in the "Emperor's New Clothing," has a preconceived notion removed our ability to see something obvious as once again obvious? I'll ask the same question one more time before moving on, why are we restricted from what our limitless minds can *potentially* invent?

    There is a short promotional film from 1940 of the well known inventor Reuben Garrett Lucius Goldberg, best known as Rube Goldberg, titled "Something for Nothing" where he describes the *impossibility* of a perpetual motion machine. He essentially goes as far to call you an idiot for even dreaming it possible and then triumphantly advertises the use of gasoline. It's all of course presented with a tinge of cartoon comedy on top of that. Make any inference you would like from that, but watching this short movie with an open mind might give you some insight as to why I'm mentioning it here. Rube Goldberg is also credited as a cartoonist and more importantly a "political cartoonist" in addition to his other accolades. I wonder if someone who creates cartoons of what can very easily, and accurately, be labeled as propaganda and clearly is on the side of Big Oil is really the kind of person we need to tell us what we are capable of as a species. This is exactly the kind of thinking that is directed right at our children when we decide to let the government (govern-mind) provide the entirety of their learning in their most crucial early years while we helplessly work as much as possible to slowly pay off a loan on land and housing we will sadly never truly own.

8

———"Each group believes its attitudes, aspirations, and music to be the natural state of affairs in the world, and for each group **it is**."———

David Reck from "Music of the Whole Earth" 1977

• • • •

If there is one reason above all others I chose to quote this book (other than the fact that it is unmatched in its particular subject matter) it is to exemplify how stunningly diverse our entire realm truly is. There is almost no limit to how much you can learn and there is certainly more than a lifetime's worth waiting in this grand place. If only we could at least start with the common ground of knowing that each and every person in this world has different ideas about how their way of living suits them as opposed to someone in a distant land, maybe then we could see what an awful thing it really is to convince entire populations that murdering as many of "the bad guy" as possible is even to be considered as an option. Babies don't jump straight out of the womb *hating* Iraq or *HATING* Russia! This is not a natural impulse and the propaganda most nations/cultures are exposed to in order to generate this mob mentality for bloodthirsty wartime customers is reason enough to question its true motives.

Is anyone still under the impression that war is NOT for a profit? A full detailed discussion here is well beyond the scope of this book but at any point during the reading of this book, my hope is that you, dear reader, will have a moment to yourself...to reflect...to get a personally generated second opinion from deep inside your heart. A potential moment of much needed clarity towards topics that have been placed in your mind a certain way to make sure you grow up to become a certain kind of person. A certain type of thinker. Built nearly from the ground up mentally to become a slave to a system that doesn't even let you know it exists.

Or does it? Does this system actually operate on such a deep psychological level that it is abundantly clear in your physical day to day that almost every single facet of your entire life from birth, at least in most of the Western world, is actually built upon a single simple goal...to make YOU into a product? YOU are currently a product. YOU fetch a fair price and with almost zero effort or knowledge of the fact, YOU are cunningly conned into clicking AGREE over and over again until YOU no longer question the motive or potential threat to your own private existence. YOU willingly give away almost all thoughts, all physical transactions, all your friends and family and everything they do with or without you. YOU are currently one of the

most valuable things on Earth. Information is in high demand. This may seem relatively obvious but why? Is it just business? Don't corporations need your corporeal cooperation for maximum comeuppance? In George Orwell's "Animal Farm" (1945), the Seven Commandments on the wall were eventually altered and no one even noticed because over time the animals forgot what was originally written. Does this sound familiar? I'm not sure if too many other people I currently know are even remotely aware of the official language and breadth of the "Constitution" or the "Declaration of Independence" or the "Bill of Rights." After being asked to AGREE over and over and over again for DECADES...how much are you actually paying attention? Once a nation's population rises past a certain number, does the percentage of fully aware individuals decrease?

The power of these types of organizations whether governmental, corporate or even at the local level is now truly being felt at the community and even family level. These groups have the power to break apart households with simple reality TV style nonsense (24 hour news cycle) that is so effective, it is almost completely unnoticed in the typical persons day to day. Much like the symbolical references that surround our entire lives, these influences are ingested without consent, without clicking AGREE and definitely without the kind of integrity you would want from someone who is in the business of trying to own YOU. Subliminal messages are abound in digital entertainment and just as much can be tucked away inside any musical entertainment you ingest as well; so whatever rituals you are tricked into on a daily basis it is no different than clicking that all too common AGREE button.

9

———"Astronomy is the external lifeless glove; correspondences is the living hand within."———
Thomas H. Burgoyne from "The Light of Egypt" 1890

• • • •

When is the last time you opened up a dictionary? Not a cell phone or internet search but a good, old fashioned big and heavy dictionary? I'm not asking to see if you are "smart," I'm asking because there is something quite peculiar going on that is unfortunately becoming a sign of the times: DEFINITIONS ARE CHANGING!! Call it an *elastic clause* if you wish. Maybe that's as good as our wonderful Federal Reserve Concept of elastic currency or perhaps you are surprised to learn this. Definitions of seemingly science-settled words like **vaccine** and **immunization** certainly changed during our most recent attempt at scaring the entire world into some twisted form of forced hibernation so why would any other words in any language or context be off the table? If you don't trust organizations who gladly make public decisions like this, why trust even ONE thing they say?

Dictionaries that are as recent as the 1960's or 70's have blatant and very obvious differences in them from much newer ones. Look farther down the chronological line and you will actually find opinions instead of definitions. One potentially surprising example is in a copy I own of the 1966 "Webster's New World Dictionary of The American Language" (American not English). If you look up the definition for Astrology the first definition states that it is "A Psuedoscience..." This "definition" is a disguise for an opinion. Much like the Wolf in Sheep's Clothing of the infamous Fabian Society Crest I would argue that almost all Main Stream Media is veiled under this very same brand of spellcasting. Many very important people consider Astrology to hold the key to plenty of life's most humongous questions. Do the Sun and Moon not have a profound effect on all things? How could the stars which travel in a uniform wheel above us, save for the North (Pole) Star, and the planets that do their own beautiful dance, the wandering stars, not also have an affect on us? This is Astrology at its most simple and also at its most profound. To call it Pseudoscience is an injustice to humanity as a whole no matter what type of Astrology you may believe in. Perhaps we should explore our lands and seas with HD **everything** before another failed attempt at the F*inal Frontier* in grainy Black and White.

I have a very interesting, and what may seem like a silly, example to make here which is aside from the fact that I do think Astrology is real and that I DO believe it can answer many often "unanswerable" questions that perplex the general population. During a recent Southern Hemisphere total Solar Eclipse which was in the middle of the night here for me in the Continental United States, All four members of my household, My Wife, our 2 very young children and I ended up falling asleep in completely different rooms of our house. No planning, no bed for some AND our 2 dogs ended up in random spots they had never slept in as well. Did this just happen naturally or were we guided by some other force? Again, perhaps a silly example but a profound one. This has never happened before or since!

Let's all take a moment to think about the 12 sign zodiac we are presented with as well. 2 sets of 12 on our manmade clocks. 12 musical notes in our manmade understanding of Western Harmony. I actually think that's cause for investigation. I think that's proof of a construct and NOT NATURAL. If, however, you are on the fence about this particular topic then have you ever thought about it in these terms. Just food for thought that is hopefully a little less abrasive then some other topics presented in this little book you are holding.

10

———"Although this publication was created to provide you with accurate and authoritative information, it was not necessarily prepared by attorneys licensed to practice law in a particular jurisdiction. The publisher (Thomson Reuters) is not engaged in rendering legal or other professional advice, and this publication is not a substitute for an attorney's advice. If you require legal or other expert advice, you should seek the services of a competent attorney or other professional."———
   DISCLAIMER from "Black's Law Dictionary"

• • • •

This may seem like a harmless and, perhaps to most, a necessary part of a Dictionary that certainly carries a lot of weight on its own in almost all Western cultures. However, if one thinks a bit deeper about this barely noticeable yet perfectly placed paragraph you may be reminded of a similar disclaimer that seems, at least to me, to be of equal importance regarding reference materials of this category. Look underneath the base of any globe. Did you know these theoretical representations of the place we supposedly spin on are absolutely "Not for educational purposes." Why in the world (no pun intended) would that be? Do maps say this? Those huge pull-down maps we all saw in grade school, do they have this disclaimer? No they do not. Why the globe then? Our glorious conquest of our immediate surroundings beyond our atmosphere are indeed set in stone are they not? With only the most comprehensive guarantees of future technological conquests guided by science and maybe a little help from a MILLIONS of dollars *per day* budget given to NASA we will certainly get there.........next decade. YOU will have to wait I'm afraid. Until you see it yourself I would think twice before letting your theological guard down. It's easy nowadays to be an atheistic Jesus or Quetzalcoatl hater, but hating NASA seems to be hitting way too close to home for most of the general populace.

   It is not our globe Earth that Atlas is holding up but a representation of the heavens above. A firmament of lights for all to see and potentially even worship because of all the life-affirming information it gives. Most learned people throughout history didn't have a globe but rather an armillary sphere in their research quarters or library. There is a major difference, and don't think for a second that "looking up" was not a crucial part of most peoples' lives in between the four corners of the Earth up until very recently.

There was even a recent movie released in 2021 titled "Don't Look Up." It is about "low level astronomers" trying to convince the "social media obsessed" public about a coming Asteroid that will destroy the Earth...and you guessed it, it's sold as a *comedy*. It's also worth mentioning that this is used as an allegory to compare this scenario to all of the "idiots" who simply refuse to acknowledge that climate change will definitely end humanity practically overnight. Perhaps it would be more appropriately labeled as a tragedy. From taking a quick glance at how much it grossed, one could also confidently label it as a FLOP. With a huge HOLYwood A-List cast and a budget just under $80,000,000 this movie grossed less than $1,000,000 at the box office worldwide and Netflix took it from there. This movie of course won lots of prestigious (and useless) awards that I won't bother labeling here but I will mention that it ended up being the 2nd most watched Netflix movie up until that time at least!

Let's take away two very important things from this staggering statistic: Firstly, MILLIONS of dollars went to people who are already worth MANY MILLIONS in order to keep certain ideas right in your face, and absolutely nobody who decided to fund this made any money whatsoever until selling it to Netflix which essentially places it on the same level of glamour that would normally accompany a "Made for T.V." movie. Secondly, if you have a Netflix account, you are helping keep this exact type of business model viable. Who funded this? Who wants to make sure these exact concepts of a sudden devolution in our modern society coupled with our willingness to completely lose track of our true physical surroundings in this realm that we have yet to fully understand stay RIGHT IN OUR FACES? This is not even mentioning that there are other recent movies with the same exact title. Let's also not forget, once again, that this Holly-Wood (A type of wood commonly used for Magic Wands) production is intended to be a comedy. The answers to these questions are manifold but for a simple and direct conclusion to gain from this digression, please refer to the title of this book.

Perhaps the title of this book is slightly misleading so please allow me a moment to finish this thought. IF your entire body (YOU) was engaged in something equivalent to a World War then I believe it could easily be labeled as dis-ease and therefore leave your corporeal self with no choice but to completely fall apart on the spot. This WAR I'm trying to bring to light, the reason for this book, is almost entirely about bringing anyone who reads it back onto solid ground. Keep your feet on the ground and keep your head in the stars. Balancing your physical and spiritual self is the only way to keep your life from becoming the enslavement that the powers who should not be are pushing for. If YOU allow your entire existence to be governed by some invisible controllers making sure that you do everything they have planned for you from the shadows, if YOU allow your mind (ment) to be governed by forces that are ever-present and yet completely unnoticed due to your lack of knowledge then you will indeed become a wage slave who has no time for yourself and certainly not for any friends or an entire family. My goal here is to make sure as many people as possible find the light in the darkness that is currently overtaking most peoples' lives.

When I was young, I didn't want to go hiking. I didn't want to go in the pool or go to the beach. I just wanted to stay home and play video games and watch Godzilla movies. Was this simply me being *just a kid*? "I'm not a plant! I don't photosynthesize! I don't need the Sun!" I would foolishly think to myself. Was that really just me being a dumb kid?! I contest that the answer is ABSOLUTELY NOT. My generation was perfectly timed with the exponential rise in visual media of all kinds from the Astro-NOT thrusting the MTV flag into the Moon, to the domination of the video game industry as a whole, especially after we crossed over into the 2000's. This is being mentioned right now to exemplify the obvious: if you are reading this and thinking to yourself "Why have I not come across even HALF of this information yet!?!" then may I be one of the first to say "Welcome to the Club." I just missed the boat on the social media explosion of the 2000's and that may have been my ultimate saving grace. Of course I had a MySpace! Of course I had a Facebook, Twitter (whoops sorry "X") and Instagram! And now even though it would actually benefit me greatly in regards to getting this book out there as well as other things, I'm having a hard time finding an excuse to utilize them. I may use some other apps and websites that I don't necessarily want to but here is another point that will hopefully place ME and YOU, dear reader, on a more level playing field. I HAVE NO CHOICE AND NEITHER DO YOU. This is our current reality. Internet Technology is a humongous win for humanity and somehow it is simultaneously a HUMONGOUS monster that is seeking to own everything about you except your physical self...for now.

11

―――"How many rivers do we have to cross before we can talk to the boss?"―――
Bob Marley from "Burnin' and Lootin'" 1973

• • • •

Could it be that all of this wonderful technology we were force fed in the twentieth and now twenty-first century with its *Blue Light Alpha Wave Enslavement* capabilities are subconsciously convincing us to keep our attention facing straight down to Hell instead of simply seeking out the many innumerable gifts we are granted by looking up and reaching a true sense of inspiration, a true sense of self and maybe even a true sense of a community of human beings that would love nothing more than to make sure we ALL succeed and are ALL happy for as long as our physical bodies will allow? Do you own YOU? Maybe. Do you own your own land and house on that very same land...maybe not. Even if "paid off" almost 100% of the human beings here in the West do not own much of anything. Regardless of ownership are you not taxed? What will it take to find an actual ownership scenario where you yourself can truly and legally claim ownership on land that is not superseded by some government body or legal insanity that has final say on any action you take with your own "property." As I've said once or twice so far...this is a conversation for an entirely separate book and many others have already done excellent work on topics of mortgages and usury.

More important of a topic for this book is how YOU have been bought and sold many times over. Your personal information. Your data. Your needs and desires. Your habits. Your bloodline. Your actual blood. YOU...YOU are a product, and once THEY convince you to become closer and closer to a genetically modified cyborg (many unfortunately already are) then all bets will be off. Nobody here is asking you to immediately move to the coldest and most dense forest you can find and snuggle up in a big fresh bear corpse for shelter. That's a death wish for most, this is about a one step at a time defense against all of THEIR obvious attempts to make sure YOU are no longer YOU.

This book is not a survival guide but rather is written as a legitimate attempt to wake up something that is laying dormant in most BY DESIGN. You may have noticed lots of words in ALL CAPS lately but as the topics become more intense, well...so does my own passion as I write this humble little book. No one person should be the "leader" of some revolt or some movement against these injustices against humanity. No one person will "save us" from the big bad wolf BUT we can all do our best to stay aware and help each other. It is not time to burn bridges with our fellow humans. Disagree with someone's viewpoint? Love them dammit!! The things I am trying to bring to light here are the reason that so many people ardently and sometimes violently disagree on easy going topics. It is now time to build bridges and to help each other bring humanity through this palpable change of ages into a place where we really can all help each other. Not with taxes or legal advice but what herbs grow best in your area and how to make sure we all have clean water and happy trees in our lives so we can ALL thrive together. Dividing ourselves into political affiliations or even by race is exactly how we will lose this "War." Hopefully it won't be bombs and guns but the ramifications for losing are far worse than death. On the more positive side of this, whatever schemes are planned, whatever maniacal and insane machinations we sense and attempt to expose in little books like this I believe that one thing is clear: THEY know WE are winning. Much like when a game of chess is won before the winner gets to call "checkmate," the loser can only prolong the final move. There is no way out for what seems like a desperate attempt at trying to convince us we NEED them. Humans are more than special, we ARE this magical realm. We ARE this place we all call home regardless of its apparent size or shape or all of the mysteries you simply cannot explain. This place is a gift for US and WE have an obligation to keep it that way.

12

―――"My Dad was rich, my Mom was good looking...and I can still play The Blues!"―――
Miles Davis from a "60 Minutes" interview 1989

• • • •

Being a musician, and also a music teacher for over twenty-five years, gives me a particular perspective of almost any topic you can think of. It may seem like this Miles Davis quote is silly but it brings to light a very important point that I comparable made early on in this book: YOU can be anything that your tiny and quite powerful heart desires no matter what conditions you were raised in and no matter what hardships get in your way. The blues was historically developed from hardships and essentially being in a place of woe. This meant many different things of varying severity but the bottom line here is that we are currently in a period of hardship. It may be more severe right now for some compared to others but any person you know or anybody you have yet to meet will agree with that. Ironically, this might be one of the only things nearly 100% of people can actually agree on.

    Just like the blues, something beautiful can come out of terrible plights. Due to technological advances and several other factors, this first few decades of the 21st Century is truly a unique time in the history of humankind. We must all take a good look around and within ourselves to make sure that every single decision we make is for the benefit of us and those around us. Even if its something as simple as your own health/eating/sleeping habits. The healthier we all are mentally, physically and spiritually then the better we all do as a collective. I believe that this book has shown some very good examples of how hard THEY seem to be trying to break us down at even those levels FROM BIRTH. We can do better and I know that we will. If the events of the past few years has not changed you in at least one very profound way I would be VERY surprised. Look around your immediate friends and family and I'm sure you'll agree that the world has already gone through a huge transmutation and it may only be the start. Maybe in an unfortunately dark yet necessary way, this most recent attempt to upend the entire population of our world thanks to invisible enemies you will never see (or ever get proof of) will finally reveal who is actually behind all of this. The Wizard of Oz quickly showed his hand once the curtain was pulled back and it didn't seem to take very much effort at all. It's always easier said than done, but change really can happen overnight. It's up to every single one of us to make sure we can all share legendary tales of our success on the other side of this shift in overall consciousness.

———"When we speak of man, we have a conception of humanity as a whole, and before applying scientific methods to the investigation of his movement, we must accept this as a physical fact. But can anyone doubt today that all the millions of individuals and all the innumerable types and characters constitute an entity, a unit? Though free to think and act, we are held together, like the stars in the firmament, with ties inseparable. These ties we cannot see, but we can feel them. I cut myself in the finger, and it pains me: this finger is a part of me, I see a friend hurt, and it hurts me, too: my friend and I are one. And now I see stricken down an enemy, a lump of matter which, of all the lumps of matter in the universe, I care least for, and still it grieves me. Does this not prove that each of us is only a part of a whole?"———

Nikola Tesla from "The Problems of Increasing Human Energy" 1900

• • • •

What is war at its core? Is it a fight for inalienable rights? Is it a contest for conquest? Is it blind murder based on blind faith? These are difficult questions to ponder on almost any level but perhaps the most important question is twofold: who actually does the fighting, the killing and consequently the dying...and who benefits? No question is answered simply and this is certainly not void of twisting someones brain into a knot if thought about for even a brief moment. The bottom line is this, we as a species are not meant to kill each other, we are not meant to take land and life from each other. That type of insanity requires a molding of the ment, a GOVERNment or perhaps a little propaganda disguised as entertainment to go along with what seems like a natural defense of ones pride and country. This deception goes a long way but it comes with a price. Whether or not you believe the little book written by Darwin that claims human evolution is indeed real (read the book before assuming), WE DO NOT GROW as a species if all we do is knock each other down to get what we want. We CAN all grow together, we CAN all help each other prosper, WE CAN ALL EXIST TOGETHER, WE CAN ALL EXIST SIMULTANEOUSLY,

WE CAN ALL SHARE THE REALM WE LIVE IN WITHOUT KILLING EACH OTHER.

Are there any active wars right now? Obviously the answer to that is *YES*. Will there be new wars after you finish this book (and hopefully pass it off to a friend)? I would say yes BUT times are changing. Human kind is becoming more KIND. Humans are starting to see right through the propaganda and manipulation instead of charging into war. Human beings are charging right through the lies on their screens and magazines instead.

There is so much hope and potential in the human consciousness that it is actually being felt by all that wish to acknowledge it. Whether or not the cover of this book looks like the apocalypse, it is meant to be anything but that and I hope reading it so far has proven this to be true. This book is a call to action and simultaneously a cry for pure and natural freedom. Freedom for ALL people. There are plenty of Humans, if you want to call them that, who wish for us to perish under our own instincts as we are casually guided to an intentional slaughterhouse of the mind, body and soul. It's not enough to just sit down and meditate while our realm burns to the ground but, as I confidently stated earlier, I highly doubt almost anyone who is willing to follow their heart is the same person they were before COVID 9-11 and THIS is where we can finally turn the page. THIS is how we get to reshuffle the deck in favor of beautiful, simple and true HUMANITY. THEY will not win if we simply follow the natural laws of NATURE and stop believing that all of the incredible things we witness on a daily basis is just some BIG BANG MIRACLE that our very own science claims to be an aberrational impossibility!! Take the time to change one thing a week towards goals you always had. Want to wait for you "new years resolution?" DON'T!! Now is the time. It is always time to realize your true potential and if we ALL do it, things will change for the better and much faster than we would typically expect.

Or so I would like to believe, I'm not going to sit here and tell you that anything is a guarantee but I can GUARANTEE that the "Planet" isn't going to take this opportunity to simple obliterate itself practically overnight if we keep having too many climate-changing, computer hating children. There's a reason we are experiencing this place and time, this era this AGE. There's a reason why the darker forces of this place are finally showing their hand and now is the

time to finally take advantage of their mistakes. The same mistakes the invading alien race or the bad guys make in any HOLYwood production. Human beings are far more than our physical selves and we will always have our home here. No magical fairy tale dinosaurs to take it back, no magical fairy tale alien species to steal it from us, no climate change disaster to kill us all off because we are "bad" for this place that was clearly created for us. No wars with guns or brain chips, just simply living the way we were always meant to.
Providing for ourselves and our surroundings while respecting every single thing we gain from it and every single thing we do with it. In other words, live just like the highly in tune race that we used to be before we somehow let THEM get a hold of everything and use our very own perfect brains against us.

14

────"When you feel as if you'd like to play something a little bit scary, a witch is a fine thing to play."────
Fred McFeely Rogers (A.K.A. Mr. Rogers) from "Mr. Rogers Neighborhood" Season 8 Episode 63, 1975

• • • •

It's funny how easily perceptions can change over time. Especially with entertainment and even more so with the entertainment you grew up with and even cherished as a child. I primarily think back to my obsession with the Godzilla franchise which are some of my clearest and earliest memories in life. Watching them now is an entirely different experience and the level of programming and propaganda in these films is in a league all it's own. This kind of intentional programming from all forms of entertainment (and even some things passed off as non-fiction) go a long way to convince entire cultures that they are living in the "right" culture, the "good guys." Certain words, as a result of this, carry some seriously heavy baggage and simply cannot be reversed until you do some very deep introspective soul surgery. One cannot help but feel duped by whoever crafts these ultimately deceptive forms of mind manipulation.

    Why don't we get the most obvious one out of the way first. Let's think of the word WITCH. What exactly do you think of when you hear this word. Say it out loud please. It doesn't have to be loud enough for the neighbors to hear, we wouldn't want them to be scared for their lives now would we? This is the crux of the matter however. Why in the world does a name/title that some of the most incredibly wonderful healers in our world associate with have to be tarnished and branded with the scarlet 'W' simply by way of our good friends King James and William Shakespeare? Have any of you read King James' (the VI and I, look it up) book "Daemonologie" from 1597. His attempt at writing in the style of Plato having a "down to Earth" discussion of how and why witches are bad people who cast evil spells and his "even if they do good with their magic, it means they can also do very bad" logic falls quite short in any literary or rational sense. It's gibberish, plain and simple. Failed logic and fictional fallacies left and right plague this tome of garbage. Yet this is the person, the one who supposedly translated the now inimitable and seemingly "world champion" status KJV Bible, we all know and reference?! *This* Bible is the one we trust? Written by someone who absolutely loves the idea of killing natural healers and midwives, the idea of murdering people who only want humanity to thrive through natural birth and holistic wellness?

Look further into this so you can come to your own conclusions but I believe it's worth mentioning that almost everything you can think of which has some stigma or overall negativity or stereotype is a construct of entertainment in any form or at least some blindly accepted cultural norm bred directly from the most basic definition of ignorance. This is the purpose of this book and its title. This "World War YOU" is fabricated and carefully cultivated so that your entire CULTURE backs up your preconceived notions about any very deep and compelling topics while simultaneously guaranteeing that you needn't do any research on them whatsoever.

This very same entertainment, often disguised as "edutainment" or even "NEWS," has effectively affected or dare I say poisoned our collective worldview in two different and equally powerful ways: One is what was just described in the previous paragraph, the cultural inculcation of anything but the truth pertaining to our vast and incredible world. The second is the simple fact that this collective entertainment world has all but left us feeling invalidated as a human being if we don't constantly ingest this paltry pandering of our dried up pineal perceptions of the world. In other words, this entertainment in various forms poisons your mind and also eats up all of the free time you could be spending learning and growing so your friends and family can hopefully be inspired to do the same.

Some of this is more of a summation of the earlier sections in this humble little book so that there is the feeling of an arc in this stream of consciousness that I present to you here. I hope that this book has given you a sense of your world that perhaps you knew was there but had not yet taken that leap of faith into the "known unknown." I also hope that this book drives you to see every single thing that comes your way in life as an opportunity. Not as an opportunity to want the lives of others like social media, advertisements and music videos do, but an opportunity to blossom into who you were *meant to be*. This is NOT assuming that everyone out there is failing because I see quite a lot of the opposite now. I mean to produce hope for those who think all is lost and that they might as well keep their fully debted and unhappy lives going just so their kids can essentially do the same. The modern technological age offers something that has yet to be seen in the more recent generations of humanity as a whole, the opportunity to learn more about the world, to learn how to do more things well and how to learn more about ourselves, Mind, Body and Soul, then we ever had. To not take advantage of that is absolutely NOT the way forward or more importantly, NOT the way out of this seemingly downward spiral presented to us. Please take the opportunity to take the chance to become YOU because YOU know it is the right thing for you, your family and the entire population of ALL human beings in ALL continents.

15

―――"Nature hath given men one tongue but two ears, that we may hear from others twice as much as we speak."―――
Epictetus A Greek Philosopher based in Rome??

• • • •

Perhaps this is a good place to end this tireless and relatively focused rant of mine. This heartfelt hamlet of personal insight and my first book (which will surely not be my last). I have been hosting my own podcast for over a year now called Third Eye Edify (ThirdEyeEdify.com) and through that style of media I have been able to open a valve of research and information I truly believe needs documentation for our kids and their kids and hopefully beyond that. This book is not an overlap but more of an intimate way to put as much information out on the proverbial table as possible. Not as a way to bombard but hopefully a way to give people that would, for example, never see my show a chance to at least be introduced to topics I wish I had heard about as a child or, of course, a growing and constantly learning adult. Trying to discover ways to fill minds with something other than manipulative mainstream GARBAGE. If you made it this far I will leave you with this...please, PLEASE, whatever you do with this information I only ask for two very specific things of you: #1 COME TO YOUR OWN CONCLUSIONS THROUGH YOUR OWN LEVEL/STYLE OF RESEARCH!! I don't know everything and I am also still humbly learning. #2 Don't blame others just because they don't agree with you, even if you are sure that you are right. This is what politics and things of that nature do...they divide us. They divide us at work, they unfortunately divide us at home and they definitely divide us at country borders. This is anything but natural. THIS IS NOT THE WAY FORWARD FOR HUMANITY!! We have ALL been duped by this corrupt system and cannot be blamed. I provided my insights in this book without forcing conclusion but based on the title, and book cover, I am sure of one thing. There is definitely a "they" and this *thing*, this *Evil Empire* is skipping over World War III and has already started WORLD WAR YOU...

• • • •

———Alway keep in mind, for more than one reason, what this obvious "product of the system" and person I RARELY agree with named *Carl Sagan* said while testifying to the United States Congress about climate change in 1985...———

"We are all in this *Greenhouse* together."

NOTES

NOTES

Don't miss out!

Click the button below and you can sign up to receive emails whenever Jorge Mesa publishes a new book. There's no charge and no obligation.

https://books2read.com/r/B-A-ZYTAB-EHVOC

BOOKS 2 READ

Connecting independent readers to independent writers.

About the Author

Music Teacher, Podcast host and Author Jorge Mesa has always had a passion for writing and public speaking. This first book is a bold and open ended look into just what makes this modern culture tick and who may be pulling the strings. If this book piques your interest then please check out his podcast and his availability for teaching along with his exciting new Bass Player University.

Read more at Jorge Mesa's site.

About the Publisher

Third Eye Edify is the brainchild of Author, Podcaster, Music Teacher and Esoteric Researcher Jorge Mesa. What started as a podcast presenting topics focused on finding out the truth about our history as human beings quickly evolved into much more. Books, News Articles, Interviews with incredible guests and a drive towards reaching as many people as possible by branching out into news and print media. Please visit the website to find out more!

Read more at Third Eye Edify's site.

Printed in Great Britain
by Amazon